Uncomfortable Truths About ADULTING

Facing Disillusionment

Uncomfortable Truths About
ADULTING

Facing Disillusionment

OLIVIA L. HARRIS

Book Cover by Olivia L. Harris

1st edition 2024
ISBN: 979-8-218-51777-9

DEDICATION

To my incredible mom, who has stood by me with love
through everything.
To my sisters, who are my best friends.
To Prothaniel Harris, Jr. for supporting me through my
writing journey.
And to my amazing children—may life bring you all the
joy and fulfillment you dream of.
This is for all of you.
I love you deeply!

TABLE OF CONTENTS

ACKNOWLEDGMENTS

Writing this book has been a journey, and I couldn't have completed it without the support and encouragement of some amazing people. To my family—thank you for always believing in me and giving me the strength to keep going.

A heartfelt thank you to my friends and loved ones who stood by me during the ups and downs of this process. Your words of encouragement meant everything.

To my literary coach, editor, and friend—thank you for all that you are and all that you do! Your guidance and expertise have made a world of difference in bringing this book to life.

To everyone who offered their insights, feedback, and inspiration, I am truly grateful. You've all played a role in helping me shape this work into what it has become.

Lastly, to the readers—thank you for allowing my words to be a part of your life. I hope this book resonates with you and helps you in some way.

INTRODUCTION

This is the third time I've rewritten this book. The first draft was too short, just a free write of my thoughts jammed onto the pages. The second draft was more polished, and I thought it had potential, but the words didn't feel like me. That's when I realized I was following these unwritten rules that I'd been applying to everything I did in life.

It's something I've always done—following these invisible rules that I believed would provide structure. My overarching thought was always: rules bring order, and without them, there's only chaos. That's what I believed for a long time. But that belief also kept me trapped inside a rigid way of living, unable to embrace the freedom I truly wanted. When I finally became aware of it, that awareness broke me apart, and I discovered a new word: disillusionment.

Disillusionment is the feeling of disappointment when something we believed in or hoped for turns out to be flawed or false. It forces us to confront the gap between our expectations and reality—a gap that often goes unspoken until we're face-to-face with it.

Adulthood doesn't always turn out the way we expected. We start by hitting the milestones laid out for us until we're inevitably cut loose to plan our own path and make our own decisions. When that time comes, we end up going in a million different directions, enrolling in the class that only experience can teach.

When we were younger, we imagined adulthood would come with freedom, success, and the satisfaction of having it all together. That's what they told us. Every year in school, one of my teachers would say, "You need to get good grades so you can get into a good college and have a good job." But no one ever mentions the unforeseen detours and challenges—the moments that leave you questioning whether you're on the right track or if you missed the memo everyone else seems to have.

I remember my first job interview, fresh out of college. It was everything I'd been working toward—a stepping stone into the adult world I'd been told was waiting for me. I had two degrees, work experience, and my hopes pinned on the idea that once I walked through that virtual door, I'd be well on my way to success. But the reality of that moment hit harder than I expected. The job, which I thought would be my ticket to the future I had imagined, turned out to be something else entirely.

A few days before the interview, I'd done my research, practiced, and prepared, just like I was supposed to. "Always prepare for interviews. Have questions ready. Work on your elevator pitch." To me, this was common knowledge, drilled into us throughout college.

Five minutes before the video call, I sat anxiously in front of the screen, telling myself, You've got this, don't be nervous. I was nervous—but I was ready. The call started off great. I had answers to every common question.

"Tell us about yourself." Crushed it.

"Why do you want to work here?" Easy.

"Tell me about a time you've faced adversity in the workplace." I could do this in my sleep.

"Can you explain your lack of banking experience?" Uh…

"I see a gap on your resume, can you explain why?" Well…

"Why should we hire you?" Oh no.

Long story short, the interview didn't go as planned. I

noticed something that threw me off balance. As I confidently answered the earlier questions, I could see the interviewer growing visibly irritated. But when the tougher questions came, the ones I wasn't as prepared for, he seemed almost satisfied. It hit me then—he was never interested in hiring me. No matter how prepared I was, I was walking into a situation I hadn't been taught to expect.

That day, I learned a few things: the world prepares us for success on a general scale but doesn't account for biases, discrimination, or other real obstacles that can stand in our way—even when we do the work.

That was my first taste of disillusionment—the realization that the adult world I had imagined wasn't quite what I'd been sold. And that was just the beginning. As I navigated my twenties, I quickly discovered that adulthood is less about having all the answers and more about learning to live with the questions. The moments we thought would define us—landing the dream job, finding love, building a life—rarely go as planned. Instead, we're left grappling with uncomfortable truths about self-worth, success, relationships, and everything in between.

This book is my reflection on those truths, the lessons I've learned the hard way, and the ones I'm still learning. You'll notice that throughout the book, there are bolded solutions— real, actionable steps that helped me move forward. These bold moments are there to help guide you through your own journey, offering a way forward when life's uncertainties feel overwhelming.

It's not a guidebook or a set of solutions. It's a mirror—an honest look at the messy, painful reality of what it means to grow up and find yourself in a world that's constantly shifting. They're not just moments that happened to me; they're reflections of experiences many of us share but rarely talk about. Because let's face it: growing up is hard, and adulthood doesn't come with a manual though most of us wish it did. But maybe, by sharing these moments with you, we can find some comfort in knowing we're not alone in the struggle.

Through my journey of growth, I've come to realize this: Adulthood isn't about reaching a destination. It's about adapting, evolving, and having the courage to face the uncomfortable truths that life throws at us.

Each chapter of this book includes solutions, acting as callouts to highlight practical advice you can apply to your own life. At the end of every section, you will encounter final takeaways, reflection questions, and call-to-actions that invite you to take real steps toward change. Lastly, we've included a sample of a personal action plan in the appendix, giving you the tools to shape your own path forward using the insights you've gained.

As you turn the page, remember that this is a space where vulnerability is embraced, and perfection is not the goal. It's about confronting the realities of growing up and learning to embrace the messiness that comes with it.

The Shattering
of
Illusions

"It is not until we lose the illusion that we can gain the clarity."

—Anonymous

1

The Journey of Self-Love

You can't love yourself through the eyes of someone else, and that's one of the toughest lessons you'll ever learn. You can fight to love yourself, work on your confidence, and reject the negative ways others try to define you. But even when you finally find peace with who you are, it doesn't mean the world will reflect that love back to you. It's a hard realization: loving yourself doesn't guarantee that others will see your worth. And relying on someone else's approval to feel loved will always leave you feeling empty.

I used to think love—whether for yourself or from others—was simple: that if you did everything right, people would respect and accept you. But the truth is, some people who say, "I love you," don't even know what love means. Others struggle to love anyone, including themselves. And the hardest part? Sometimes, the more you start to appreciate yourself, the more you realize how little love or understanding you've actually received from others.

> Learn to affirm yourself. Practice daily affirmations, like "I am enough" or "I deserve love and acceptance." Remind yourself that your value does not depend on others' opinions.

Self-love is supposed to be the key to self-worth, but the journey to get there isn't without pain. My first lesson in this came at an early age when I didn't even know what self-love was—only that I felt like I didn't deserve it.

It happened in kindergarten, after nap time. Our classroom had a small playroom with toys like play kitchens and pretend setups for "house." The teacher let the kids who woke up early go in and play. One day, four girls and three boys were up, and we decided to pair up and play "house." But there was one problem: there were more girls than boys.

One girl, with light skin and long, curly brown hair, took charge. She was the leader, and she decided who would be paired as husbands and wives. I remember watching her go around the group, pointing to each person as if she had the power to determine everyone's roles. But when she got to me, she stopped, looked me up and down, and skipped over me without a word. She paired everyone else up, then turned to me and said, "Since you're the ugliest one here, you can be the dog."

I didn't know how to respond. I was five years old, confused, hurt, and embarrassed. All I could manage to say was, "Okay." I curled up on the mat, pretending to be the dog as the others played. But inside, my chest ached. I lay there with silent tears streaming down my face, trying to understand why she had said that to me. It was the first time I realized that beauty—or the lack of it—mattered, even to kids. That day changed me. It taught me something I hadn't known before: people could decide your worth based on things you had no control over.

That experience introduced me to something else I hadn't felt before—anxiety. From that day forward, I felt nervous whenever I met new kids, worried that they might say something hurtful about the way I looked. That underlying fear became a constant presence, and it shaped how I interacted with people. I was always on edge, walking on pins and needles, making sure our conversations didn't touch on anything that might lead to a discussion about looks. I became so focused on avoiding the topic of beauty that I lost out on connecting with others.

I've realized now that comparing ourselves to others— whether in childhood or as adults—can cause deep wounds. When I stopped measuring myself against others, I started feeling more at peace.

Stay focused on your journey.
Comparison only leads to self-doubt.

For years, I let one person's opinion define me. I convinced myself that everyone who met me thought the same way—that I was less than because of my darker skin. I started to believe that beauty wasn't meant for people like me, and with that belief came the slow erosion of my self-esteem. I relied on my friends to tell me I looked "okay," because I didn't believe I could ever be more than that.

The truth is, many of us see ourselves through the eyes of others, and it can be devastating. When someone labels you as ugly, fat, or undesirable, those words attach themselves to your identity. I've been told countless times that "it gets better" or "it's just high school." But as I grew into adulthood, I realized something even more unsettling: it doesn't get better by much. Some adults are even crueler than children.

This experience made me hyper-aware of how I looked at any given time. I fell into a cycle of seeking validation from others—a cycle you don't want to find yourself in. When you seek validation from others, you lose control over who you become. After that day in kindergarten, I became obsessed with asking my friends and family, "How do I look in this?" It was a question I came to hate, but I needed the answer.

I spent too much time worrying about what other people thought about me and how I looked. This concern was so intense that when I was out with anyone, I would become a rigid version of myself, making sure I sat, ate, laughed, and spoke in certain ways. It was exhausting, and it led me to cancel many plans.

My weight, particularly after giving birth to my last child, loomed over me like a dark cloud. It dominated my thoughts more than anything else and drove me to unhealthy behaviors, like skipping meals to lose weight quickly. Even after losing the weight, I wasn't satisfied. Post-divorce, I bought my first SUV, feeling a mix of excitement and dread about having to post a photo on social media for the dealership's promotion. Despite trying to mentally prepare, the photos turned out as badly as I feared. Even after losing seventy pounds, I couldn't see past my weight when I looked at those pictures, feeling huge and shrinking inside.

I tried to retake the photos to see if there was a difference. There was, but it was minimal. So, I strapped on my waist trainer that night, told the kids to go play, and exhausted myself running up and down the stairs until my legs gave out. The next day, I was sore and filled with regret, unable to take even a single step without pain.

I've lost close to 100 pounds, and I once believed that reaching this goal would make me feel more accepting of myself. With the importance the world places on size, I thought I'd be doing myself a disservice if I didn't lose the weight. But all it did was earn me a few extra compliments—"Oh wow, you've lost weight"—and endless questions about how I did it. I had this goal of achieving a body like the "baddies" people praise today, and I thought it would give me some sense of validation. But it felt emptier than I could have ever imagined.

What I learned through this experience is that society's emphasis on beauty is an illusion. The world tells you that if you look a certain way, if you lose the weight, if you fit into its ideal, then happiness and acceptance will follow. But that's a lie. In reality, those fleeting compliments did nothing to fill the void inside. I had achieved the external goal, but the internal struggle remained the same. It was a moment of profound disillusionment—realizing that no amount of validation from others would ever make me feel whole. Self-love could never come from meeting external standards; it had to come from within. This is where the illusion of self-worth, built on outside approval, began to crumble for me.

> Choose to be around people who respect you for who yor are, and see your worth, even when you are struggling.

Looking back, I realize how important it is to surround yourself with people who uplift and support you. Your environment plays a huge role in your healing.

During my weight loss journey, I kept telling myself that I didn't care what others thought—that I was doing it to get healthy and stay around for my kids. And while I truly do believe in the importance of health, I can't deny that, deep down, I cared very much what the world thought of me. I thought that losing weight would somehow make me more acceptable to others and to myself.

When most of the weight came off, I realized I had become the very thing that used to hurt me. I posted pictures on social media to show my progress, telling myself that I wanted to motivate others who were struggling with the same battle. But if I'm being honest, some of it was for validation. I wanted to show the world that I had heard its criticism, that I had "fixed" what they said was wrong. I had internalized the world's expectations without even realizing it.

In my disillusionment, I learned that the idealism society builds around weight and beauty standards is a façade. Yes, the world might care about appearances, and many of us face discrimination or low self-esteem because of it. But the truth beyond the illusion is this: there is no single standard of beauty. Everyone has different tastes, and the more we cling to some universal idea of what beauty should look like, the less control we have over how we feel about ourselves, how we live, and how we navigate the world.

To get back to the real point, self-love has always started with the self. A person who truly loves themselves enough to accept who they are can't be made into what the world wants them to be. That's the disillusionment I've faced—thinking that external change would bring internal peace, only to find out that peace comes from accepting myself exactly as I am.

We don't like to admit it all the time, but the standard of beauty is real. There are unspoken rules about how we should look, and there always have been. People say, "It's not about how you look," and while that rings true on a deeper level, vanity dominates the surface. We have to look deeper to recognize that even those we consider the most beautiful among us have serious insecurities about their appearance. Everyone does, but when it comes to first impressions, we are judged by vanity— and that's where our biases lie.

It's unfair how something so external and broad is used to define something as deep and intimate as our identity. Self-worth

---

You are not defined by your past or by what others
say about you. Forgiveness is part of self-love.

---

should be personal, not shaped by external forces. But even if we don't choose the criteria others use to judge us, our actions often align with the way we perceive our own worth.

An important part of my journey has been learning to forgive myself and let go of past mistakes. Allow yourself to move forward without the weight of those labels. Remember, healing takes time, but every step brings you closer to loving yourself fully.

Learning to love yourself starts with dismantling the beliefs about yourself that don't align with who you want to be. For me, I had to stop practicing colorism against myself. Colorism, often within the same racial or ethnic group, means darker-skinned individuals are discriminated against, while those with lighter skin are favored.

It has taken years for me to see my skin as a part of me, not a curse. For a long time, I wished I was lighter, wished I was thinner, wished I looked like the girls on social media who seemed to have the life I wanted. Comparison is the enemy of self-love, but we all do it. We compare everything—our looks, our cars, our homes, even our shoes.

Being the middle of five girls, I often compared myself to my sisters—and so did everyone else. Boys liked to compare us, and I often lost because I was darker. This only pushed me further into a narrative about myself that someone else had created.

I didn't realize that the real disease wasn't my skin, but the thoughts I had built up over the years. My true power emerged when I finally understood that I had never disliked darker skin—I believed Black is beautiful. But before I could fully nurture that belief, I had been told otherwise.

I had to break the cycle. I had to be intentional about deciding what aligned with my identity and what didn't. What didn't fit, I discarded. With those old thoughts gone, I made room to discover myself—to grow into the person I was meant to be. Self-love is the most important thing we can get right in adulthood. It stands behind everything we do. It influences how we choose our partners, how we raise our children, how we pursue our dreams, and even the companies we choose to work for.

Building self-love takes time. For me, the journey is still ongoing because I'm not perfect, and I still have growing to do. Lean into yourself with positivity and start now. No one has the right to impose their negativity onto you. Mistakes can be corrected, and you can choose today to reject the labels that don't belong to you. Toss them away and stand in the truth of who you are. We're breaking the cycle of allowing ourselves to live broken.

Today, as I stand, I am proud to be who I am. I love my skin, and I don't care who doesn't. If I could go back in time, I would hug my younger self and tell her not to let others' opinions define her. I would remind her that people's perceptions will always differ, and if someone's perception isn't for her, let it be for them. The most important opinion of who she is and how she looks is her own. Be strong, little Livi. I love you.

As I began to understand the illusion of external validation, I realized that knowledge itself often carries a similar burden. The more I learned about myself and the world around me, the heavier that knowledge became. Knowledge, like self-love, doesn't always make things easier. It can complicate life in ways I never anticipated, revealing truths I wasn't always ready to face. In the same way that we chase self-love, we often chase knowledge, thinking it will provide the clarity we seek—but what happens when knowing more only adds to the weight we carry?

The uncomfortable truth is this: true self-love cannot be found in the validation or approval of others. Society will continue to push its narrow standards of beauty, success, and worth, but they are illusions. The real work begins when we let go of the need for external approval and start the journey of embracing ourselves fully, flaws and all.

Only then can we truly love ourselves—without needing the world's permission to do so.

CALL TO ACTION

Take a moment to list 3 things you love about yourself and reflect on them daily.

TIME TO REFLECT

Reflection: When was the last time you prioritized your own well-being?

Reflection: What are some beliefs about self-worth that no longer serve you?

FINAL TAKEAWAY

Self-love is a journey, not a destination, but it's the most rewarding journey you'll ever take.

2

Chasing the Weight
of Knowledge

"Knowledge is power"—we've all heard it countless times. For much of my life, I believed it. I thought that learning more would grant me control over my future, that knowledge would open doors and bring freedom. But as I grew older, a different question began to emerge: Power for whom? In our society, the people who hold real power are the ones shaping the systems we live under—governments, corporations, institutions. They understand these systems inside and out, and they control what the rest of us are allowed to know.

The more I learned about the world, the more I realized that knowledge can become a burden, especially when you're powerless to change the things you uncover. It's not that I've become a conspiracy theorist, but I've come to sympathize with them. I understand the helplessness they feel when they start peeling back the layers of truth. It's like knowing how something works but being utterly powerless to stop it.

To put it simply, it's like eating a hotdog. Growing up, I loved pork—hotdogs, bacon, ham. I never thought twice about what was in them. Every now and then, someone would say, "Do you even know what's in that hotdog?" And I'd say, "No, and I don't want to know." Because once I knew, I'd probably never eat one again. That's the weight of knowledge. Sometimes, ignorance really is easier.

> Not all knowledge needs to be pursued. Learn to prioritize what will serve your growth and well-being

It's important to understand that we are not powerless in deciding how much information we allow to shape our perspective.

I've avoided looking too deeply into certain things for the same reason. And it's not just about food—it's about life. If we truly understood the systems that control our lives—the things we consume, what we're taught, the choices we think we're making—it would be hard to keep going without feeling weighed down. The more you know, the less free you feel.

A harsh truth about adulting is that not everyone or everything can be trusted. Decisions, whether personal or those made by institutions, are often driven by interests we aren't aware of. More often than not, those decisions benefit the people in control, not us.

True power doesn't just come from knowledge—it comes from controlling the choices available to us. Imagine I gave you three career paths to choose from. You'd feel empowered, thinking you have control over your future. But in reality, I've already shaped the outcome by deciding what your options were in the first place. That's the illusion of choice—a controlled game, where those in power determine our paths long before we even realize it.

I remember when disillusionment hit me. I was sitting in my house, alone. My divorce had just been finalized, and the kids were with their dad. I was working on my laptop with *Heroes* playing in the background. As the characters navigated their lives with superpowers, I found myself daydreaming about what power I'd want if I could choose. Super speed? Super strength? Maybe the ability to talk to machines like Micah?

But then it hit me—none of those powers would actually fix my life. Even if I had super speed, I'd still have to wake up early, slog through the day, and work until five. My situation wouldn't magically change. That's when the weight of reality started settling in.

As I sat there in my quiet house, I began questioning everything. I cried, and I'm not sure if it was because of my divorce or something bigger—something deeper. I thought about systemic inequality, racism, and how my hard work seemed to matter so little in the grand scheme of things. The more I knew, the heavier it all felt.

Focus on small actionable steps you can take to create change in your personal life or community.

By shifting focus to what you can control—whether it's influencing your environment, supporting local efforts, or educating others—you can ease the burden and prevent feeling powerless.

My first real encounter with how deeply the system is rigged came when I noticed the changes happening in my own neighborhood. At first, everyone was excited. The city was building new developments—tearing down old schools and buildings to make way for a multi-million dollar downtown project and a sleek new transit system. On the surface, it seemed like progress.

But I couldn't shake the feeling that something was off. I kept hearing the word "investors," and I knew investors always expect a return on investment. So I wondered, how would this city, with its high crime rates, worn-down houses, and lack of jobs, possibly repay these investors? Then I learned that the new housing being built wasn't for the existing residents—it was for professionals, priced at market rate. That's when I started connecting the dots.

Through research, I learned the word for what was happening: gentrification. What I had once thought were improvements were actually signs of displacement. They were closing predominantly Black schools, pushing low-income families out, and making room for wealthier residents. This wasn't progress for the community—it was a slow and deliberate erasure of it.

I dug deeper, learning about the history of systemic racism in housing policies, redlining, and how Black neighborhoods were cut off from economic opportunities. I uncovered how the "projects" were designed to contain us, how warehouses were strategically placed in Black neighborhoods to offer low-wage jobs, and how housing contracts excluded Black people from owning homes in certain areas. It was all by design—carefully constructed to keep us in place.

When powerlessness feels overwhelming, focus on advocacy that challenges harmful systems.

Then it got personal. I saw the mayor use eminent domain to take a couple's property. They showed up to plead for their land, explaining that losing it would mean financial ruin for their family. The mayor didn't care—he wanted that land for a new restaurant. I felt powerless, knowing there was nothing I could do to stop it.

Collective action is often one of the strongest ways to create change.

I tried to warn people in the community about what was happening. I tried to explain that the excitement over these "improvements" was misplaced—that we were being pushed out of our homes. But no one listened. Now, I see it happening. Property taxes have skyrocketed, power and water bills are higher, and public housing is quietly evicting residents without replacing them. The same story I had read about in books and watched in documentaries was now unfolding before my eyes.

This experience pushed me further into learning about the systems that have oppressed people of color for generations. The more I knew, the heavier it became. It was as if knowledge itself was a burden—one that couldn't be lifted, no matter how much I wanted to believe otherwise. Looking back, I've realized that formal education never prepared me for any of this. It wasn't designed to. School wasn't about teaching us to think critically about the systems we live in—it was about making us into the people society wants us to be. It was set up to train us, not to open our eyes.

Rows of desks, bells signaling when to move—everything about school felt like we were being trained for something, but not for real life. It's like that Bible verse, "Train a child up in the way he should go, and when he is old he will not depart from it." That's what the education system is doing: training us to accept the world as it is, without question.

> Critical thinking and independent learning are crucial tools in navigating the complexities of the world.

None of the knowledge I've gained about systemic control, oppression, and power came from school. It came from my own research, my own curiosity. And that's the unsettling part— the education system wasn't designed to open our eyes. It was designed to keep them shut.

Seeking out diverse sources of information, questioning what is presented, and continuously educating ourselves can help combat the limitations of traditional systems.

In the beginning, before the weight of it all hit me, it was exhilarating to uncover these truths. I felt like I was discovering something few people knew. It was like watching a tornado from a distance—exciting, almost fun, because it was too far away to seem real. But as I learned more, the tornado got closer. The excitement turned to fear. I was no longer watching from afar—I was in the storm.

The real burden came when I realized there was little I could do to change things. The systems I had uncovered were so deeply entrenched, so cleverly designed, that no amount of knowledge on my part could dismantle them. And that's the frustration of having knowledge. You understand the problems, but you can't fix them. You can warn others, but that doesn't mean they'll listen.

What frustrates me most is knowing how far back these systems go and realizing that we'll never know the full story. None of us will. Knowledge isn't just a collection of facts—it's a narrative, and narratives can be manipulated. The truth gets buried under layers of time, lies, and distortions, and it feels unfair. Knowledge, which should be liberating, can be used as a tool of control.

The more I learned, the more I realized that someone holds the key to knowledge—and that person holds the power. But who is it? Who decides what we get to know? It feels like chasing a puzzle where half the pieces are missing. And yet, we keep searching, hoping that one day we'll piece together enough to see the bigger picture.

> **Accept that you won't have all the answers and focus on acting with the information you do have.**

I believe that truth can't be fully hidden forever. I believe in God, and with that belief comes reassurance that He is ultimately in control. No matter how much the world tries to hide, there are things God will never allow to remain concealed for long. It's that belief that keeps me searching for wisdom, even when the weight of knowledge feels unbearable.

In the end, what I've learned is this: the more you know, the more you see the cracks. Knowledge opens your eyes to the systems that control us, but it doesn't give you the power to change them. That's why too much knowledge can feel like a burden. It strips away the illusion of control and forces you to confront the fact that many of your decisions were shaped by forces beyond your reach.

Knowledge offers opportunities for personal growth and understanding.

Instead of focusing solely on the weight of knowing, we can strive to use what we learn to make informed, intentional decisions, even within the constraints of the systems around us.

The uncomfortable truth is that knowledge, while often hailed as the key to power and success, can also weigh you down. It doesn't always lead to clarity or control—sometimes it reveals just how little control we really have. The more we understand the systems around us, the more we see how they're rigged against us.

CALL TO ACTION

Identify one belief you've outgrown and release it with grace.

TIME TO REFLECT

Reflection: How has your pursuit of knowledge shaped your current perspective?

Reflection: What beliefs have you had to unlearn as you've grown?

FINAL TAKEAWAY

True wisdom comes not just from knowing, but from recognizing the limitations that knowledge reveals and learning to navigate within them.

3

Sink or Swim

Adulthood hits before you know it, and unlike childhood or adolescence, there's no gradual transition or preparation for it. You just wake up one day and realize that you're on your own, expected to make decisions that will impact your future, whether you're ready for them or not. There's no manual, no clear path, and no one is there to guide you through the critical moments. You're left to figure things out, often through trial and error, and sometimes those errors come with consequences you have to live with for years.

One of the first times I really felt the weight of adulthood was when I had to walk to work through a snowstorm. I was working at the movies, which was about 15 or 20 minutes away by car. It had just finished snowing—a lot. My coworker and I were stuck; neither of us had a ride. We figured our boss would understand. It was a snowstorm, after all, so we called to let her know we'd be late. Her response was simple: "Get here, or you both won't have a job anymore."

That moment hit me like a ton of bricks. I felt a sense of panic I hadn't experienced before. It wasn't just the panic of losing my job; it was the realization that, as an adult, there are no excuses. The safety nets of childhood were gone. When you're a kid, you have allowances for bad weather or circumstances beyond your control, but as an adult, those allowances disappear. You're expected to show up, no matter what.

We didn't have a choice, so we bundled up and started walking. The streets were covered in snow, and we were exhausted before we even reached the halfway point. Every step felt like a struggle. The cold wind cut through our coats, and the snow on the ground made it hard to walk. But we kept going, because we knew the alternative—losing our jobs—was not something we could afford. I remember thinking, "This is adulthood. This is what it means to be grown." I had to make a choice between walking through a storm or facing the consequences of not showing up. Either way, I was responsible.

> Prepare for the unexpected. Build resilience
> through small daily challenges so you can
> handle the bigger storms life will throw at you.

That experience taught me something important: there's no leeway when it comes to adulthood. I had a choice, but I didn't really have a choice. If I said no, the consequences would fall squarely on me. No one was going to pick up the slack for me anymore. No one was going to step in and fix things if I couldn't handle them. I was on my own.

One of the lessons here is that adulthood often comes with tough decisions.

Before this, I had always thought my boss was rooting for me. She had seemed like someone who wanted me to succeed. But that day, I realized she wasn't as concerned about me as I thought. She wasn't interested in my future; she was focused on hers. Her job was to keep things running smoothly, and if I didn't show up, it would affect her bottom line. It was a harsh wake-up call. I learned that people in positions of authority—bosses, managers, even teachers—aren't necessarily there to help you succeed. Many of them are just doing their jobs, and sometimes that means putting their own needs before yours.

It took a while for me to come to terms with that lesson. For years, I kept making mistakes, learning the hard way that adulthood doesn't come with built-in safety nets. There's no one to catch you when you fall, no one to give you a second chance when you mess up. And when things went wrong, I had to fix them—sometimes without even knowing how. I felt lost, constantly scrambling to figure out what to do next.

It's essential to recognize that while authority figures may not always be invested in your success, you can create your own support systems.

> Surround yourself with mentors who can offer guidance when you need it, rather than relying on traditional authority figures.

The anxiety that came with that realization became a constant companion. I began to second-guess every decision I made. I'd write out multiple plans for every situation, trying to cover all my bases, but it never felt like enough. I became paralyzed by the fear of making a wrong move, afraid that one mistake could set off a chain reaction that would ruin everything. Even the simplest decisions, like where to live or what job to take, became monumental obstacles in my mind. The more I overthought, the harder it became to move forward.

For a long time, my finances were a mess. I wasn't saving anything, and I spent money as soon as I got it. Payday loans seemed like a quick solution whenever I ran out of cash, but they only dug me deeper into a hole. I was also making terrible financial decisions in other areas. I remember my 21st birthday—I was finally old enough to go to the casino, and I thought it would be fun. At first, it was. I started winning, and that rush of excitement made me feel invincible, like I could keep winning and never lose. It was a dangerous feeling because it gave me the illusion that I was in control, that I could do whatever I wanted and always come out on top.

Educate yourself on basic financial literacy—budgeting, saving, and understanding credit.

But that illusion didn't last. I kept going back to the casino, convinced that I could win more, but instead, I lost money—money I didn't have to lose. I wasn't saving, I wasn't budgeting, and I wasn't thinking about my future. I was just trying to escape the stress of adulthood by indulging in the fun parts, like spending money, eating out, and doing whatever made me feel good in the moment.

I wasn't thinking about the long-term consequences because, quite frankly, no one had taught me how. Growing up, no one sat me down to explain credit, savings, or how to build a career.

I was figuring it out on my own, making mistakes and learning from them, but the cost of those mistakes was high.

These foundational skills can prevent costly mistakes and provide stability in times of uncertainty.

My relationships with my family also began to suffer. My sisters started to see me as someone who was always asking for money, always making reckless decisions. I became the irresponsible one—the person who couldn't get it together. It hurt, but I didn't know how to change. I was spiraling, caught between wanting to fix my life and not knowing where to start.

My mental health took a nosedive. I was disillusioned with life, feeling like nothing I did would ever work out. It was a strange combination of depression and denial. I tried to drown out my feelings by focusing on the funnier parts of life, doing things I can't imagine doing today. I told myself that this was just the way life was, that this was what adulthood looked like— constant struggle with occasional moments of escape.

But eventually, it all caught up with me. I fell behind on rent, and my landlord told me she was trying not to kick me out. She saw potential in me, and instead of evicting me, she called me into her office. I'll never forget that conversation. She gave me a deal—$85 a week for the rest of the year, as long as I stayed in school. That deal saved me. It gave me a chance to breathe, to think about my life and what I wanted for the future. It was a turning point.

Getting help is not a sign of failure; it is a step toward growth.

In difficult times, it's important to ask for help and seek out opportunities for grace. Sometimes, there are options you may not have considered, and asking for assistance can open new doors.

I started taking things seriously. I reached out to the payday loan companies and asked if I could get on a payment plan, just like my landlord had done for me. To my surprise, they agreed. Slowly but surely, I began to get my finances in order. I wrote out all my bills, set up payment plans, and worked hard to get everything current. I even used a credit repair company to fix my credit. For the first time in my life, I felt like I was in control.

But even then, there were limits. No matter how responsible I became, certain systems were still stacked against me. When it came time to find a new apartment, I couldn't qualify because I didn't make three times the rent, and the fact that I was an independent contractor didn't help. It was frustrating. I was doing everything right, but the system wasn't designed for people like me—people who didn't fit neatly into the boxes society had created.

I found myself bouncing from one family member's house to another, feeling like I didn't belong anywhere. I had a car, but I didn't have a stable place to live. I was back at square one, struggling to find my footing in a world that didn't seem to have room for me. The anxiety crept back in, and I felt more lost than ever. Then I met someone—a guy who would eventually become my husband. Our relationship moved fast, and before I knew it, I was married with four children. But even that journey wasn't as smooth as I'd imagined. We tried for two years to get pregnant, and it didn't happen. I never knew about infertility growing up—I had been taught all through high school to avoid pregnancy, so I thought once I was ready, it would just happen. But it didn't.

When we finally did get pregnant, I was in a car accident at six months. It was a terrifying experience, but nothing prepared me for what happened next. At 29 weeks, I developed severe preeclampsia and had to have an emergency C-section. My daughter was born prematurely and stayed in the NICU for eight weeks. It was one of the hardest times of my life. No one had ever told me that these kinds of things could happen. I had

---

Be flexible and prepared for the unexpected.
Have a contingency plan.

---

always thought pregnancy was simple—get pregnant, have a baby. But I wasn't prepared for the possibility of complications, and I definitely wasn't prepared for the emotional toll it would take on me.

Those experiences—infertility, the NICU, and everything in between—taught me that life doesn't follow a script. No matter how much you plan or prepare, there will always be things you can't control. There's no manual for dealing with the unexpected, and adulthood is filled with unexpected challenges. The anxiety I had before only intensified. I became so careful, so focused on doing everything right, that I forgot how to live. I was responsible, but I wasn't happy. I was working hard, but I wasn't enjoying life. I had become so consumed with being an adult that I lost sight of what it meant to be human.

It took me a long time to realize that adulthood doesn't have to be defined by constant struggle. Yes, there are challenges, and yes, there are things that will go wrong. But that doesn't mean life has to be miserable. I've learned to find joy in the little things—like taking my kids to the park or watching them smile without a care in the world. I've learned to appreciate those moments because they remind me that life is more than just bills, work, and responsibilities.

I often questioned the path I had taken. I worked hard for years, earning degrees in information systems and business, only to find that neither degree guaranteed me a job. After years of school, the only job I could find was as a customer service chat agent, making $17 an hour. It wasn't the career I had envisioned, but it allowed me to work from home and take care of my children, which was a blessing in itself.

But even with that blessing, I realized that the version of success I had been chasing wasn't what I really wanted. I thought owning a house, getting a car, and having a career were the ultimate goals, but when I achieved those things, I still didn't feel fulfilled. It wasn't until I started writing this book that I realized what my real purpose was. Writing has always been my passion, but for so long, I ran from it because I didn't see how it could lead to a stable life. Now, I'm working on my first fictional series, and for the first time, I feel like I'm living my purpose.

> A fulfilling life is not solely about achieving external milestones. Find your purpose.

Finding your purpose, especially through activities that bring joy and meaning, can provide a deeper sense of satisfaction. Focus on what truly excites you, even if it doesn't fit the traditional model of success.

> Strength grows not in the absence of challenges,
> but in how we respond to them.

The truth is, adulthood is what you make of it. It's not about following a set path or achieving a checklist of milestones. It's about finding what makes you excited to wake up in the morning. It's about working on your passion and living your purpose, even if it doesn't look like what society tells you it should. Adulthood doesn't come with a manual, but that doesn't mean you can't write your own.

The uncomfortable truth is that adulthood doesn't come with a manual, and you're often left to figure things out on your own. There's no blueprint for how to navigate the sudden responsibilities, challenges, and unexpected twists that life throws at you. But what I've learned is that adulthood is what you make of it. You have to take control of your own story, even if it means learning through trial and error. The mistakes you make don't define you, but they do teach you. And while there will always be things outside your control—like unexpected hardships, financial struggles, or health crises—how you respond to them shapes the path forward.

Adulthood may not come with a guide, but you have the power to create your own roadmap.

Resilience, the ability to bounce back from adversity, is often what separates those who thrive in adulthood from those who get stuck. Psychologists explain that resilience isn't about avoiding struggles, but about developing the skills to face them head-on. This includes problem-solving, learning from mistakes, and practicing self-compassion when things go wrong. Adulthood may come with unexpected storms, but building resilience means we don't have to face them unprepared.

CALL TO ACTION

Identify a past moment where you felt overwhelmed and reflect on how you overcame it.

TIME TO REFLECT

Reflection: What "sink or swim" moments have defined your adulthood?

Reflection: How do you navigate the weight of responsibility when no one is guiding you?

FINAL TAKEAWAY

Focus on what you can control, find joy in the small moments, and stay committed to your purpose.

4

The Mirage of Success

The thrill of success is addicting. It can give you money, fame, respect—everything society tells us to strive for. I chased those promises too. I wanted a big house for my children, financial stability for my family, and recognition for my hard work. But even as I reached these milestones, the emptiness lingered.

I realized something deeper was missing. Material things, no matter how grand, just sit there. My house, my car—they filled up space, but they couldn't fill the voids.

True success, I learned, comes from living with intention—not from the size of your paycheck or the admiration of others. When you stop chasing superficial goals, you create space for what really matters—your relationships, your passion, your personal peace.

A key part of redefining success is understanding that material items will never provide long-lasting fulfillment.

As I started questioning what really mattered to me, I

> Focus on what brings true meaning to your
> life—relationships, personal growth, and
> emotional well-being.

realized that true success isn't about things you can buy or own. But to get there, I had to face a deeper fear: the fear of failure. As adults, we're often too afraid of falling short of expectations—whether they're our own or society's. That fear of failure keeps us chasing superficial goals because we think we'll be seen as "successful" if we just follow the rules. But if you're too scared to fail, you're too scared to truly succeed.

By reframing failure as an opportunity for growth rather than an endpoint, you can push beyond superficial goals and embrace a path that aligns with your personal values.

Adulting means redefining success, even if it means rejecting what others think is important. It's about realizing that the things that bring real fulfillment—like spending time with my children, being present in the moment, and doing something I love, like writing—can't be measured by money or status. It's taking risks with your time and energy to pursue what actually matters to you, rather than what you're told to value.

The world, however, doesn't always value these things. Society celebrates success it can monetize—status, wealth, fame—and sees anything else as laziness. But I've learned that real success comes from living with intention, not just chasing the next material reward. If you let the fear of failure stop you from chasing what you really want, you'll end up succeeding at things that don't matter and failing at what does.

Chasing an Undefined Dream

Many of us grow up chasing a version of success that we never truly define for ourselves. We adopt the goals, expectations, and dreams that we've seen around us—whether from family, friends, or what we see in the media. This leads to a disconnect, where we strive for something without fully understanding what it means to us personally.

Reflect on your personal goals, desires, and values, rather than accepting what others tell you success should be. This internal clarity will guide you toward more meaningful achievements.

Without that personal clarity, success can feel like running toward an invisible finish line. We may achieve goals, hit milestones, and check boxes that look impressive on the outside, but internally, something feels missing. The sense of accomplishment we expect never fully arrives, and it's often

Take time to define what success looks like for you.
Confront your fear of failure to find true success.

because we haven't asked ourselves what success actually looks like for us as individuals.

That was my journey through multiple degrees and certifications. I spent countless sleepless nights staying awake to achieve the goals I thought were mine. But when I reached those milestones, I realized I was left feeling empty. I was chasing a narrative of success that wasn't truly mine. It was a story I had absorbed from the world around me.

I thought I wanted the big house, the title, the respect, and the admiration. But when I achieved those things, the sense of fulfillment I expected never came. People congratulated me, but every time I said "thank you," I felt disconnected from what they were praising me for. It's not that I didn't work hard—it's that I was working toward someone else's idea of success.

When we follow someone else's definition of success, it's easy to feel like an imposter. You might reach the goal, but if it doesn't resonate with you on a deeper level, the reward feels hollow. That's the heartbreak of chasing an undefined dream.

> If chasing goals leaves you feeling empty, take a step back and ask whether they align with your desires. Realign your path.

You work tirelessly, only to find out that what you were chasing wasn't really yours to begin with.

To avoid this disconnect, be intentional about setting goals that reflect your values. Regularly reassess your ambitions and ensure they're in line with who you are and what you want out of life.

So what does it mean to define success for yourself? It means stepping back and asking the hard questions. What do I actually want? What makes me feel alive, fulfilled, and at peace?

When you chase a dream that is truly yours, the effort becomes more meaningful because you know why you're doing it. This realization didn't happen overnight for me. It took time, introspection, and even disappointment to get there.

But once I understood that success has to come from within, everything changed. I realized that success is not about external markers, but about finding alignment with your own values and

God-given purpose.

The Conditioning of Society

From an early age, society begins to shape our understanding of success. We're taught that success looks a certain way—wealth, status, fame—and that these are the things worth pursuing. These ideals are reinforced constantly, through the media, our educational systems, and cultural norms. Rarely are we encouraged to pause and question whether these societal definitions align with our own beliefs or values.

This conditioning leads many people to chase external markers of success without ever asking if they truly resonate with what they want out of life. The same narratives are repeated over and over—success is a big house, a high-paying job, financial security. If you don't meet these markers, society often treats you as if you've failed. The pressure to conform to these standards is immense, and it often leaves people feeling trapped in a cycle they didn't choose for themselves.

> Shift your mindset. See failure as a learning tool not a final judgment.

This conditioning doesn't stop in childhood—it follows us into adulthood. One of the most damaging aspects of this societal pressure is the fear of failure that it instills in us. From a young age, we are taught that mistakes are something to be ashamed of. We're punished for spilling a drink or scolded for getting bad grades. Instead of being given the chance to learn from our failures, we are made to feel that failure itself is unacceptable.

This creates a deep fear of falling short, and that fear stays with us long after we've grown up.

By shifting our mindset around failure, we can begin to see it as a learning tool rather than a final judgment. This change helps reduce fear and allows us to take risks that bring personal growth.

As adults, the fear of failure leads many people to procrastinate—not because they don't want to try, but because they are terrified of the consequences of failing. Procrastination in this sense isn't laziness; it's a way of protecting ourselves from criticism, rejection, or humiliation. If we can avoid trying, we can avoid failing. And the more society criticizes us for our failures, the less likely we are to try again.

> Develop a growth mindset by encouraging yourself and others through positive reinforcement.

What makes this cycle even worse is how society often reinforces behavior through negative means. Growing up, we are more likely to be punished for our mistakes than praised for our successes. This emphasis on punishment creates anxiety and discourages risk-taking. When people are constantly criticized or punished for not meeting a standard, they become less willing to take chances, try something new, or push beyond their comfort zone. Over time, this creates a kind of paralysis—people are too afraid of failure to attempt success.

But it doesn't have to be this way. Positive reinforcement—encouragement, support, acknowledgment—has the power to inspire people to keep trying, to learn from mistakes, and to grow.

*Celebrate small wins and use them to build
your confidence for larger risks.*

When people are motivated by positive reinforcement, they are more willing to take risks and challenge themselves. The truth is, the stress caused by constant negative reinforcement makes it impossible for people to function at their best. That's the real illusion society creates: that failure is something to fear when, in reality, it is a natural part of growth and success.

The system benefits from keeping most people in fear of stepping outside the norm. This keeps society running smoothly, with only a few breaking free to achieve what is celebrated as success. Take the banking system, for example. It thrives on keeping people in debt, paying off loans and mortgages for decades. If everyone suddenly woke up and decided to withdraw all their money at once, the banking system would collapse. The system needs people to stay dependent on it to survive, and it's designed in such a way that most people never question how trapped they've become.

But the truth is, society only keeps us down if we choose to live by its unwritten rules. The more aware we become of these patterns, the more we can shape our beliefs apart from what society tries to impose on us. You don't have to accept the definitions of success, failure, or risk that were handed to you. You can choose to live by your own standards.

An uncomfortable truth is that society is designed to keep most people in place while lifting a select few. But disillusionment doesn't have to be a dead end. It can be the starting point for real change. The more you understand the illusions society places on you, the more you can break free and define success on your own terms.

Emotional freedom is an empowering
form of success.

Success as Freedom

For many, the idea of success is tied to external achievements—wealth, power, and recognition. But for me, true success is about emotional freedom. It's the ability to control your emotions, to decide how you want to feel at any given moment, no matter the circumstances. This kind of freedom is the most powerful form of success because it allows you to make decisions with a clear mind, free from the weight of stress, anxiety, or fear.

Cultivate emotional resilience by practicing mindfulness, learning to manage stress, and maintaining a balanced perspective in challenging situations.

When I was laid off from my job in 2023, I experienced firsthand how emotionally tied I was to my role. I felt lost, confused, and, above all, angry. I had worked so hard, taking on student loan debt, dedicating myself to the job, only to find that it could be taken away in an instant. I realized then that my sense of self-worth was too dependent on my job. The traditional concepts of working and education had been sold to me as a path to success, but in reality, they were about making someone else more money. And when I was no longer valuable to them, I was discarded.

This experience taught me that success has to be about more than job titles or income. Success, for me, became about emotional resilience. It's about knowing that when something leaves—whether it's a job, a title, or an opportunity—you're still okay. You don't fall apart because you've built your foundation on something deeper than what society says defines you.

A person who can control their emotions is someone who can navigate life on their terms. They can decide to stay calm, be patient, and remain confident, even in uncertain situations. This kind of freedom allows them to choose who they want to work for, and to walk away from any situation that doesn't serve them—without fear. They don't chase after every opportunity, nor do they panic when one slips away, because they understand that their worth isn't tied to a single moment or decision.

In fact, people who embody success as freedom are the biggest assets to any company, even more so than those chasing traditional success. They have the patience to play the long game, to see beyond the pressure of instant gratification that society constantly pushes. They can make clear-headed decisions, free from the emotional highs and lows that so often drive others to burnout or failure.

Cultivate your internal strength.

In contrast, societal success is fickle. It makes you believe that by following the "rules"—climbing the ladder, working harder, accumulating more—you'll find lasting success. But the truth is, societal success comes and goes as it pleases. It feels like luck when you get it and a gut punch when you lose it. It's wishy-washy, unpredictable, and often beyond your control.

Success based on emotional resilience remains steady, regardless of external circumstances. When you cultivate this internal strength, your sense of worth remains constant, even when life throws unexpected challenges your way.

Success as freedom, on the other hand, is steady. It doesn't matter if opportunities come or go, because you've built a foundation that can't be shaken by external events. You are the constant in your own life, no longer at the mercy of what happens around you.

An uncomfortable truth is that society conditions us to believe that success is something we achieve through external validation. But real success, the kind that lasts, comes from within. When you have emotional freedom, you are in control—no matter what comes your way.

Success, as society defines it, is often a mirage—something we chase without understanding what it truly means to us. We are conditioned to believe that status, wealth, and material achievements are the markers of success, but the truth is that these external rewards can feel hollow when they don't align with our personal values. Real success comes from breaking free from societal expectations.

Success as freedom is about having the power to navigate life on your own terms, to make decisions based on what fulfills you—not what others say you should value—and the time you have to enjoy it. The real uncomfortable truth is that society sets us up to chase a version of success that keeps us tied to external validation, but once you understand this, you have the power to redefine success for yourself.

Redefining success is just one part of a larger journey. As we move through adulthood, the ideals we once held—about fairness, justice, and how the world should work—start to break down. The certainty we had in the systems and values we were taught to believe in begins to crumble under the weight of reality. In the next chapter, we'll take a closer look at how this breakdown of idealism affects not just our sense of success, but our understanding of the world around us. It's a hard truth we all face, and it's central to the disillusionment that comes with growing up.

The uncomfortable truth is that society conditions us to chase a superficial version of success—one tied to material achievements, status, and external validation. But real success comes from within. It's about emotional freedom, aligning your actions with your true values, and finding fulfillment in the things that matter most to you. The path to success is not defined by societal standards but by your ability to live intentionally, embracing failure as part of the journey and shaping a life that resonates with your personal sense of purpose.

CALL TO ACTION

Write down one way you can redefine success based on what truly matters to you.

TIME TO REFLECT

Reflection: What external markers of success have you chased, and how have they affected your sense of fulfillment?

Reflection: How does your current definition of success align with your personal values?

FINAL TAKEAWAY

Real success comes from within. Be intentional. Embrace failure as part of the journey.

5

The Illusion of Choice

As adults, we often feel that we're steering the direction of our own lives, making decisions that shape our success and happiness. We pick where we want to live, the careers we want to pursue, and even how we spend our free time. But as I've come to realize, many of the choices we think we're making aren't really choices at all. From government programs to our jobs, our lives are often shaped by a set of pre-approved options handed to us, and we're left to choose from what's already been decided. This is the illusion of choice.

One of the clearest examples of this illusion is the welfare system, particularly food stamps and public housing. On the surface, these programs are designed to help people in need, offering a lifeline to those who are struggling. But beneath the surface, they act as traps that keep people dependent on the system. Take food stamps, for example. To qualify for them, your income must fall below a specific threshold. The moment you earn just a little too much—just enough to cross that line—

you lose your benefits. But that small income bump is hardly enough to make up for the loss of assistance. So, people stay stuck, choosing to work less or remain at jobs that won't push them over that limit because the risk of losing their safety net is too great.

Imagine being a single parent, working while going to school, and barely scraping by. You get a raise at work, just enough to disqualify you from food stamps, but not enough to cover the increased cost of groceries. What would you do? For most people, the choice is simple—they'll find a way to keep their income under the threshold. They'll take fewer hours, turn down promotions, or simply accept that they can't move forward. The system that's supposed to lift them up is the same one holding them down.

Build a support network to help you navigate and break free from the restrictions that programs create.

While these systems offer essential support, it's important to find ways to push beyond these limitations. Seek financial education, look for transitional programs.

Public housing is another example of this illusion. These units, often located in low-income neighborhoods, are meant to provide affordable housing for families who can't afford to live elsewhere. But there's a catch: the more money you earn, the higher your rent becomes. So, once again, people stay stuck. The idea of working harder to earn more sounds good in theory, but in reality, every extra dollar goes straight to rent, leaving families no better off than before. Public housing wasn't designed to help people escape poverty; it was designed to keep them in it.

What's worse is how deeply the system infiltrates every aspect of life. To receive food stamps, Medicaid, or public housing, you have to submit paperwork that details every part of your financial situation—your income, household size, expenses— everything is monitored and controlled. You're forced to check in regularly, proving that you still "deserve" the assistance. It's not just about helping people—it's about controlling them. If you make a mistake, if you forget to submit a form or fail to disclose a side income, you risk losing everything.

To navigate such complex systems, seek out legal aid, community organizations, or support groups that specialize in helping individuals understand their rights and obligations. This knowledge will help you avoid common pitfalls while on these programs.

When you grow up in these systems, you're taught that this is what life is. Your choices are limited by design. There's no dream of moving into a better neighborhood or earning enough to live comfortably. The options are simple: stay where you are, or risk losing it all. It's no wonder that so many people who depend on these systems feel trapped, like they'll never escape the cycle of poverty. The illusion of choice isn't just about what's offered—it's about what's withheld.

Seek out legal aid, community organizations, or support groups to help avoid pitfalls.

I've spoken to so many people over the years who dream of owning a home, of breaking free from the system and finally feeling like they've "made it." But when I ask if they believe they'll ever reach that goal, the answer is always the same: "Not in this lifetime." Why? Because they don't know anyone who owns a home, and they don't know how to achieve that dream themselves. The path has been laid out for them—stay in the system, follow the rules, and don't try to push too far outside of it. If you do, you'll be penalized.

The hardest part of living within this illusion is that it's not just about the choices you make—it's about the mindset you inherit. For those of us raised in public housing or who grew up on food stamps, the idea of striving for something better feels almost pointless. When the system tells you over and over that you're only worth what they say you are, it becomes harder and harder to believe in your own potential. Why would someone try to reach for something more when they've been conditioned to think that they can't have it?

Surround yourself with possibilities that defy
the narrative of "staying stuck."

Challenge limiting beliefs and mindsets. Seek mentors, coaches, or success stories from people who've broken free from similar systems. This mindset is passed down from generation to generation. In public housing, it's common for a mother to raise her children in the same unit for years. Then, when those children turn 18 and have kids of their own, they qualify for their own unit. It's one of the few things that can be "passed down" in these communities—a government-subsidized home, not wealth or opportunity. For many, this is seen as a win. The daughter gets a unit, the family stays close, and the cycle continues. But the truth is, this isn't passing down anything of value—it's passing down dependency.

Break generation cycles of dependency with financial literacy and self-reliance.

Start teaching financial literacy and self-reliance within families to break generational cycles of dependency. Passing down knowledge and skills can be a greater inheritance than any physical asset.

When I think about the illusion of choice, I'm reminded of a conversation I had with a friend in high school. She lived in a wealthy part of town, and one day she took me to visit her home. As we drove through her neighborhood, I couldn't believe what I was seeing. Her high school was massive, much bigger than mine, and when I pointed out the size difference, she casually mentioned that they had six gyms. I was shocked. My entire high school could have fit inside one of her gyms. It was a stark reminder of how the choices we think we have are shaped by our circumstances. I didn't choose to go to my high school, and she didn't choose to go to hers. Those decisions were made long before we were even born, based on where our families could afford to live.

When I asked my friend why there weren't any Black families in her neighborhood, she told me, without hesitation, that it was because it would lower property values. I was in tenth grade at the time, and I didn't fully understand what she meant. But it stuck with me, and as I got older, I realized that the segregation

I saw wasn't just about where people lived—it was about access to opportunity, to education, and to wealth.

The same can be said for corporate America. As a Black woman navigating the corporate world, I quickly learned that the choices available to me weren't the same as those available to others. No matter how qualified I was, no matter how hard I worked, I always felt like I had to prove myself—like I had to show that I belonged in spaces that weren't designed for people like me. The higher I climbed, the more I realized that the rules of the game weren't fair. Success wasn't just about working hard or being the best—it was about who you knew and how well you fit in with the people who already held the power. And those people didn't look like me.

Do not view success as an exception but a path.

The illusion of choice extends into every corner of society. The jobs we're allowed to have, the schools we're allowed to attend, even the neighborhoods we're allowed to live in—all of these choices are pre-determined by forces outside of our control. And yet, we're told that if we just work hard enough, we can have it all. But the truth is, the system was never designed for everyone to succeed. Success is a luxury reserved for a select few, and the rest of us are left to keep the system running.

This isn't just true for people of color or those living in poverty—it's true for everyone. The illusion of choice touches every part of life. Think about the options you're given in any situation. When you apply for a job, you're presented with a set of positions that have already been created, with salaries that have already been decided. When you go to the grocery store, you're choosing from the products that have been stocked on the shelves by companies that control the supply chain. Even the homes we buy are built by developers who decide where and how communities will be structured.

> Advocate for equal access to resources and
> education so that more people have the tools to
> break free from societal limitations.

For those of us who do manage to break free from the system, it often feels like we've won some kind of lottery. But the reality is, our success doesn't mean the system is changing—it means we've become the exceptions that prove the rule. We're held up as examples of what's possible, but in truth, our stories are used to perpetuate the illusion that anyone can make it if they just try hard enough.

The uncomfortable truth is that many of the choices we think we have are controlled by systems designed to limit our potential. However, by challenging these limitations, cultivating a mindset of self-reliance, and redefining success on our terms, we can begin to break free from the illusions that hold us back.

CALL TO ACTION

Evaluate a recent decision— what factors influenced your choice?

TIME TO REFLECT

Reflection: In what areas of your life have you felt your choices were limited?

Reflection: What new possibilities have opened up through disillusionment?

FINAL TAKEAWAY

Cultivate a mindset of self-reliance. Redefine success on your terms and break free from the illusions holding you back.

Section Two

Navigating the Depths of Disillusionment

"Your journey is a process of becoming, and each truth you uncover leads you closer to who you truly are."

—Unknown

6

The Breakdown of Idealism

The systems we were taught to trust are often built to uphold comforting lies, not real fairness—beliefs that help us navigate the world with a sense of safety. We're told that hard work leads to success, that justice is fair, and that if we follow the rules, we'll be rewarded. These ideas form the foundation of our worldview, shaping how we see ourselves and others. But as we grow older, we start to see cracks in those beliefs. The world isn't as simple as we were led to believe, and that's where the breakdown of idealism begins.

I used to believe in the fairness of the world. The idea that if you worked hard, you'd be rewarded and that justice would prevail. But life taught me differently.

The disillusionment came when I realized the rules we live by don't apply equally to everyone. It was a hard truth to face, but in that moment, I learned that success and fairness aren't guaranteed. And that's where true growth begins.

Recognizing that justice isn't always fair helps set more

realistic expectations about the system. Instead of relying solely on external systems, seek out opportunities for advocacy, community action, and legal reform to create change.

Justice, as it's often applied, isn't about fairness at all. It's about who can lie the best, who has the most persuasive lawyer, and who can manipulate the biases of a jury. Everyone knows that people of color receive harsher sentences than others for the same crimes, but despite this knowledge, little has been done to address it. How is that fair? Is justice even about fairness, or is it about maintaining control? Systems like these seem to operate on fear, much like the film *A Birth of a Nation* portrayed, where fear is used to control narratives and keep certain people in power.

Recognize that justice isn't always fair.

The case of Trayvon Martin really hit me hard. When I heard about it, I thought it would be an easy case. A man went after a kid, the kid was killed, and naturally, I expected the man to go to jail. But that's not what happened, and I was shocked. Trayvon's case opened my eyes to how little has changed. People of color are still seen as criminals, still viewed as threats, just like in the days of slavery.

The case sparked a widespread movement, where we began to chant "Say Their Names." But the truth is, there shouldn't be a world where we have a growing list of people to chant for. The list of names is long, and it keeps growing:

- Rodney King
- Trayvon Martin

- Michael Brown
- Eric Garner
- Tamir Rice
- Sandra Bland
- Philando Castile
- Breonna Taylor
- George Floyd
- Daunte Wright
- Elijah McClain
- Tyre Nichols...

I'm sorry.

It chills me to my bones that I have to one day sit my children down and tell them that the police, who they currently see as protectors, may not protect them simply because of their skin color.

Find ways to stay involved in activism or community to channel pain into action.

These aren't just names; they're people who lost their lives because of the color of their skin. Every time I hear another name added to this growing list, I feel myself shut down a little more. The numbness takes over, and now my reaction has become: "It's just life." But that's what makes it even more painful—because it shouldn't be.

While acknowledging the emotional toll of these injustices is important, finding ways to build alliances and educate the next generation are key ways to combat systemic injustice.

This breakdown of idealism doesn't just stop with the justice system. It also seeps into our education. I used to love school. I was the kid who woke up every day excited for the structure and the learning. But as I got older, I noticed that the same people I went to school with—those who worked just as hard as I did—ended up jobless or barely scraping by. We were told over and over that if we got good grades and went to college, we would get good jobs. But that wasn't true for many of us.

> Education is important. It is also essential to learn practical skills like personal finance, networking, and emotional resilience.

The jobs I thought I'd have a chance at after high school didn't come. Then I went to college, and the same thing happened. It was only after I graduated and struggled to find a stable career that I realized something: school only prepares you to pass school. It doesn't prepare you for the real world. We weren't taught how to navigate job markets, how to deal with debt, or how to handle life's challenges. We were just told to follow the script, and things would work out.

Taking control of your learning through self-education or mentors can help bridge the gap between academic achievement and real-world success.

I spoke about this in a previous chapter, but the realization crushed me. There's such a big emphasis placed on school, learning, and achieving. No one likes to suffer and sacrifice for it to amount to nothing. Now, I have over $100,000 in student loans, but no one prepares you for high unemployment rates, inflation, or the rising cost of living—factors that make success difficult no matter how educated you are. It felt like no matter how much I accomplished, the world around me was changing faster than I could adapt.

The worst part was that there was no one I could complain to about this. So, I went to God. I contribute all of my success to Him because, without His guidance, if I had only gone off what the world taught me, I wouldn't be able to write this book today. Now, I view education as just another product the world wants to sell us and make a profit from. Understanding that success is not just worldly helps reframe what really matters in the long run.

And then there's homeschooling. Only my oldest daughter tried traditional schooling. When she was in kindergarten, she could already read words like "macroeconomics." She would score in the top 99 percentile when they did their student testing,

---

Spiritual reflection can provide comfort when external systems fail to deliver expected results.

---

but she hated school. Her class was going over the ABCs every day, and she was bored. Since she hated public school, I decided to homeschool her. Once I did, she soared, and her siblings followed close behind, learning from her.

She found a love for art and technology. She's now started coding and creating digital animations. She loves learning and reading. When I removed the limits of traditional schooling, she naturally gravitated toward the subjects that excited her. I no longer had to push her to do her work or read because, with the interest being there, she saw learning as an advantage, not a chore. She doesn't complete work just for a grade—she completes it to understand.

Allowing children to explore their interests beyond traditional schooling can lead to a lifelong love of learning.

> Disillusionment is painful, but it can be a
> doorway to rebuilding a more authentic,
> grounded sense of self.

Consider offering kids educational alternatives that fit their passions rather than adhering strictly to conventional pathways.

The hardest part about disillusionment is that it doesn't just affect how we see the world—it affects how we see ourselves. Our worldview is built on the core beliefs we've held since childhood, and when those beliefs start to break down, we're left questioning everything. For me, it all came crashing down at once. The justice system, the education system, the belief in hard work paying off—it all fell apart. I was left feeling lost, isolated, and even depressed. It was a breakdown of my entire idealistic view of how the world should work, and I wasn't sure if I would ever come back from it.

Use these moments as opportunities for self-reflection, and redefine your values and beliefs based on your own experiences rather than societal expectations.

But here's the thing: I didn't come back as the same person. I found a new version of myself. One that's more realistic, more grounded in truth. I still believe in fairness and justice, but I also understand now that those things don't exist in the ways we were taught to believe. They have to be fought for. My new worldview is built on the uncomfortable truth that not everything is as it seems, and sometimes, there's nothing we can do about that.

Disillusionment can feel lonely, like you're the only one waking up to the reality that the world isn't what it pretends to be. But in truth, more people are living with some form of disillusionment than we know. It's that feeling of going through life on autopilot, waking up each week and wondering why life feels so hollow. It sucks to go through this, but the upside is that once you wake up, you can live more authentically. You can live in a way that suits you, not the version of you that society expects.

In the end, the breakdown of idealism isn't the end of the world—it's the beginning of living in truth. And while that truth may not be as comforting as the lies we were raised on, it's far more powerful.

Break down the comforting lies that society has built and replace them with an authentic and grounded version of yourself, guided by your own values. In the end, this truth will carry you forward, even when the systems around you fail.

CALL TO ACTION

Let go of one unrealistic expectation today and replace it with a grounded belief.

TIME TO REFLECT

Reflection: What idealistic belief have you had to let go of in adulthood?

Reflection: How has your perception of fairness or justice shifted over time?

FINAL TAKEAWAY

Choose to live in truth. Guide your own values. Truth will carry you forward, even when systems fail.

7

Disillusioned in Love

Love is one of the greatest feelings in the world, likely one of the first we experience as babies, and it usually happens naturally. One of my most cherished memories of feeling true love was when I first held my newborn daughter on my chest.

Born at twenty-nine weeks, she was the tiniest baby I'd ever seen, weighing only two pounds and three ounces. I was terrified to hold her; she was so fragile. As I sat in a chair, the NICU nurses helped me with skin-to-skin contact, propping my feet up and assisting with removing my shirt. I was still sore from the C-section and preeclampsia, swollen and uncomfortable.

The nurse placed a thin yellow blanket over me and carefully picked up my daughter. I remember feeling shaky as I watched this tiny baby being placed on my chest. Her skin was warmer than I expected. Once she was nestled against me, I placed my hand, which covered her entire back, on top of her and pulled the blanket over us. My heart swelled as she snuggled up, wiggling her little body under my hand and making the cutest little sounds.

At that moment, I was introduced to a new dimension of love. When I finally brought her home, weighing four pounds, I felt nervous again. I doubted my ability to be a good mother. But when she arrived at my apartment, it was as though I instinctively knew what to do.

Love guided me through feeding her, changing her diapers, and waking up every few hours, despite my exhaustion. It gave me the strength to keep her safe and healthy. Love was the force behind the actions that formed our bond.

Let love guide you through life's challenges.

By trusting your instincts and recognizing the quiet strength love provides, you can overcome your self-doubt. But as I've learned through life, love is much more complicated than what I felt in those early moments. Love can also be toxic, and many of the beliefs we have about it are shaped by society and media, especially romantic movies.

We grow up watching stories of love at first sight, of fate bringing two people together against all odds, and we believe that's how it's supposed to be for us. We're taught that love is magic, that it's supposed to be easy, and that we'll know it when we find it.

My own experiences with love were deeply influenced by these romanticized narratives. From childhood, I believed that finding a soulmate was the most important thing, that love was supposed to be this all-consuming, fairy-tale experience. But reality isn't like the movies, and I've had to unlearn many things I thought were true about love.

One of my earliest experiences of this misguided idea was in elementary school when I thought I was in love with a boy in my grade. It seemed magical at the time. The attention he gave me, the way he made me feel seen—it was enough for me to believe I had found something special. I carried that idealized version of love into adulthood, thinking love was supposed to be full of sparks, excitement, and fate pulling two people together.

Looking back, I see I was clinging to an idea of love that wasn't real. I was holding on to infatuation and calling it love. But as I got older, I learned love is not always magical. Sometimes, love is quiet. Sometimes, love grows over time. And sometimes, the people we think we love are not the ones who are right for us.

Falling out of love or realizing that our idealized notions of love don't align with reality is a common part of human experience. Many relationship experts suggest that love isn't just about chemistry or passion but about mutual respect, trust, and shared values. Learning to navigate love involves recalibrating expectations—recognizing that no relationship is perfect, but real love is built on understanding and emotional commitment. Recognizing red flags and knowing when to let go are vital steps in protecting our mental and emotional health.

Real love is steady, based on mutual respect,
and takes time to grow.

Love isn't defined by dramatic moments or magical feelings.

I always fell for people who weren't good for me. It didn't matter how many red flags they showed; as long as I felt those butterflies, nothing else seemed to matter. I was chasing excitement and being wanted, ignoring what should have made me run in the opposite direction. But love isn't about butterflies—

Healthy love is built on mutual respect, communication, and shared values.

---

it's about something much deeper.

As adults, we learn relationships are about more than just love. They're about compatibility, respect, communication, and mutual care. Love alone isn't enough to sustain a relationship. You can love someone with your whole heart, but if that love isn't returned, if respect and trust aren't there, then it's not the kind of love that will last. Real love requires effort and intentionality. It's not always easy, but it's worth it when it's healthy. Prioritize these qualities to form lasting relationships.

One of the uncomfortable truths about relationships is that love can't fix everything. I used to believe that if I just loved someone enough, they would change. But love doesn't work that way. No matter how much you love someone, you can't make them into the person you want them to be. You can't force someone to love you the way you deserve. True love is about partnership, about two people choosing to be there for one another, not just when it's easy, but especially when it's hard.

Another truth I had to learn was that self-love plays a huge role in the relationships we choose. In Chapter One, I talked about the importance of loving yourself, and that lesson applies here too. You can't fully love someone else until you've learned to love yourself. If you don't value yourself, you'll end up in relationships where your love isn't valued either. You'll give and give, hoping the other person will see your worth, but you need to see it for yourself first.

Real love is about trust. It's about giving someone the power to hurt you and trusting that they won't. It's about vulnerability and knowing that even when things get tough, the person you love will be there—not to tear you down but to help you grow. Love is pain, but it's not intentional pain. Real love is understanding and kindness, even when things aren't perfect.

As I grew older, I learned that my idea of love needed to change. I stopped chasing the butterflies and started looking for something real. I began to understand that love isn't about grand gestures or fairy-tale moments. It's about the quiet, everyday acts of care and attention. It's about showing up for each other, not just when things are easy but when things are hard. It's about

---

Self-love is essential. Learn to value yourself.
When you do, you will attract relationships
where your love will be truly valued.

---

choosing to love, even when it's not convenient.

The uncomfortable truth about love and friendship is that neither is as simple or magical as we've been led to believe. Both require more than just emotion—they demand mutual respect, trust, and effort from both sides. Whether in a romantic relationship or a friendship, you can't force love, and you can't hold onto connections that don't reciprocate the same care and effort you give. In both, self-love plays a vital role. You have to love and value yourself first before you can expect to have healthy, meaningful relationships with others.

Real love and real friendship aren't about constant excitement or grand gestures—they're about consistency, honesty, and the willingness to show up, especially when it's hard.

The hardest lesson of adulthood is understanding that not all relationships are meant to last, but the most important relationship you'll ever have is the one you build with yourself. Learning to be okay with being alone is essential because it frees you from chasing unhealthy connections and helps you appreciate the relationships that truly matter.

True love lies in the everyday acts of care and consistency, honesty, and the willingness to show up. Choose love even when it's hard.

CALL TO ACTION

Reflect on a relationship that no longer serves you— how can you move forward with clarity?

TIME TO REFLECT

Reflection: How has your understanding of love changed over time?

Reflection: What relationships in your life have shaped your beliefs about love?

FINAL TAKEAWAY

Value and love yourself before you expect to have healthy, meaningful relationships with others.

8

The Impact of Grief and Loss

Friendships, love, and the way we view relationships shape so much of who we are. But one thing that often gets overlooked is the impact of grief and loss. We talk about love and connection as if they'll last forever, but the reality is that nothing is permanent. In adulthood, we're confronted with this truth time and time again, whether through the loss of a loved one, the end of a relationship, or even the death of a dream. The disillusionment that comes with facing loss is profound, and it changes how we move through the world.

A few years ago, I lost someone very close to me, someone who became part of my family when I was in first grade. My sisters and I met him through church, where he took us every Sunday. He was a doctor and, in so many ways, the best adult we knew. He wasn't overly strict or distant like some adults. He laughed with us, taught us about God, and even convinced my mom to let him take us out for ice cream on school nights—a rare privilege growing up.

Looking back, I see that knowing him made my childhood better. He brought balance and wisdom to our lives without forcing it on us. He didn't try to control us, but he was always there, guiding us through the little moments that shaped who we were becoming. He gave me my first taste of what adulthood could be like when he let me and my sister have a "job" at his office. I was so excited to sit at his desk, answer the phones, and write down messages, pretending to be a professional.

At the end of the day, we even negotiated our wages into ice cream instead of money. It's funny to think about now, but those small moments left a lasting impression on me. They shaped my desire to be part of the working world and gave me a glimpse of what adulthood might look like.

> Identify what matters most—whether relationships or personal goals—and devote your energy there.

As I grew older, life got in the way. We moved, and though he visited throughout our teenage years, I eventually lost touch. Life became busy, and my focus shifted to my marriage, my job, and building my own family. It wasn't until I received the news of his death that I realized how much I had missed out on. I hadn't reached out in years. He had never met my children, and they never got the chance to know him. The news hit me hard. I was consumed with regret for all the missed opportunities to reconnect.

But grief isn't just about the pain of losing someone—it's about how it forces you to rethink your relationship with time. We go through life assuming we have all the time in the world.

We tell ourselves there will always be another opportunity to visit, to call, to reach out. But when loss strikes, it's a harsh reminder that time is slipping away faster than we realize.

> Focus on mutual relationships where there's equal effort. Don't feel obligated to maintain relationships that drain you emotionally.

For me, the experience of loss has made time feel like it's speeding up. It feels like every day, I hear about someone else who has passed. And in those moments, I find myself wanting to reach out more often, to tell the people I care about how much they mean to me. But at the same time, loss has reshaped the way I make decisions. I no longer feel the need to chase things that don't bring me real fulfillment. Life is too short to be unhappy, to spend time chasing goals that don't have meaning.

Grief forces us to be intentional with our time. One of the most important lessons grief has taught me is to value my time. Instead of rushing toward success or material goals, I've learned to slow down and focus on what really matters. I've stopped stressing about work the way I used to. I no longer let small inconveniences upset me or derail my peace of mind. And most importantly, I've redefined what success looks like for me. It's no longer about money, achievements, or status. Now, success looks like inner peace, spending time with my children, and building a life that feels aligned with my values. Grief changes your priorities in a way that nothing else can. It strips away the noise, the distractions, and the meaningless goals, leaving you with a clearer sense of what truly matters.

But grief also brings disillusionment. As adults, we know on some level that nothing lasts forever, but losing someone close makes that reality sink in. There's no escaping the fact that life

---

Focus on nurturing inner peace and emotional resilience.

---

is fragile, that people we love will one day be gone. It's a truth we all know but rarely confront until it's forced upon us. The disillusionment of loss doesn't just come from the absence of the person—it comes from how it reshapes our understanding of time and permanence.

When we're young, we live in a state of naivety, believing we have all the time in the world to build the life we want and to connect with the people we love. But loss shatters that illusion. It teaches us that time is fleeting, moments are precious, and nothing is guaranteed.

Since losing him, I've become more selective about the relationships I invest in. I've come to value mutual connections—those that are balanced. Before, I spent too much time worrying about what people thought of me, trying to mold myself into someone they would accept. It was stressful and draining. But now, I've learned to let go of that. If someone doesn't want to invest in a relationship with me, I no longer take it personally. I've learned to let things be, to accept that not every relationship will last, and that's okay. I find peace in knowing the connections meant to last will, and those that fade are simply making space for more meaningful ones.

Loss also forces you to think differently about your goals. For me, it made me realize how much of my life was filled with distractions—mindlessly scrolling through social media, wasting time on things that didn't add real value to my life. After experiencing loss, I started cutting out the noise. I became more intentional with my time, focusing on what really matters and letting go of everything else. It's been a process of re-prioritizing, of learning to live with purpose instead of just going through the motions.

Grief has no timeline, and healing takes time.

One of the biggest lessons grief has taught me is that while we can't control the losses we experience, we can control how we respond to them. I've learned to find peace in the present moment. I don't stress about work the way I used to. I don't get upset over little things. I've shifted my focus toward personal growth—not in the traditional sense of climbing a career ladder or chasing success, but in terms of emotional resilience and inner peace. I'm not focused on forming new relationships, and I'm okay with being alone if I never get married again. I've learned to find contentment in my own company, and that has been one of the most freeing realizations of my adult life.

Loss, as painful as it is, makes you more intentional. It forces you to slow down, to pay attention, and to live with a greater sense of purpose. I no longer stress about what I can't control. Instead, I focus on what I can—my own growth, my peace, and my well-being. It's not about achieving external success anymore. It's about cultivating inner peace that can't be shaken by the ups and downs of life. And while grief is something I'm still working through, I've found that it has made me more resilient, compassionate, and aware of what truly matters.

Grief is a deeply personal process, but it's also one of the most universal human experiences. Psychologists note that while grief manifests differently for everyone, common stages—

Let go of things that don't truly matter and become more intentional with time and energy.

---

such as denial, anger, bargaining, depression, and acceptance—can provide a framework for understanding our emotions. Coping mechanisms vary, from journaling and talking to loved ones, to seeking therapy or engaging in spiritual practices. Allowing yourself to grieve without feeling pressured to 'move on' too quickly is key to finding healing and eventually reaching acceptance.

Grief and loss reshape our perspective, forcing us to confront uncomfortable truths about time, relationships, and ourselves. They remind us that life is fleeting and nothing is guaranteed. Through that pain, we can find clarity. Grief doesn't follow a timeline, and healing is gradual, but through it, we can discover a deeper sense of peace, purpose, and resilience.

CALL TO ACTION

Take a moment to write a letter to someone you've lost, expressing what they meant to you.

TIME TO REFLECT

Reflection: How has loss influenced your understanding of life's impermanence?

Reflection: In what ways has grief reshaped your priorities?

FINAL TAKEAWAY

Loss teaches us to cherish what we have and prioritize what brings real meaning.

9

Coping with Disillusionment

Disillusionment hit me hard. It crept in slowly, but when it took hold, it left me feeling lost. There were days I couldn't see a way out.

Disillusionment occurs when the beliefs and expectations you've held for a long time suddenly collide with reality, and you realize that what you thought was true no longer makes sense. It's not just disappointment—disillusionment runs much deeper. It's about losing faith in something you once believed was solid, only to find out that it's fragile, or worse, a lie.

One way to manage disillusionment is by accepting that it's a natural part of growth.

It happens to everyone at some point, whether we're talking about relationships, careers, or personal ambitions. The key is to see it not as a failure but as a process of waking up to a new reality.

Instead of focusing on the loss of what you once believed, shift your mindset toward what you can learn from this change.

Disillusionment can happen to anyone, regardless of their status, wealth, or success. In fact, it can be even more jarring for those who seemingly "have it all" because the gap between their expectations and reality feels wider. For example, both Anthony Bourdain and Robin Williams, despite their public success, faced internal struggles that led to tragic outcomes. Their stories remind us that success and material wealth don't necessarily protect us from disillusionment—and that's why it's important to focus on inner fulfillment, not just outward achievements.

The seriousness of disillusionment cannot be overstated. It's a full-blown shift in worldview that can cause a crisis of identity and hopelessness. In severe cases, it can lead to depression or destructive behaviors.

> Identify what matters most—whether relationships or personal goals—and devote your energy there.

One way to begin healing is by practicing self-compassion. Rather than blaming yourself for not having all the answers, be kind to yourself and recognize that this process is a normal part of growth. Allow yourself the space to grieve the loss of your previous beliefs.

Take small, intentional steps toward regaining control.

When faced with disillusionment, people often feel isolated and powerless. Instead of trying to fix everything at once, focus on small actions that bring you comfort and stability, whether it's spending time with loved ones, reconnecting with a passion, or journaling to process your thoughts. This helps create a sense of movement, even if the path forward feels unclear.

Another step is to redefine your idea of success and happiness.

Identify what matters most—whether relationships or personal goals—and devote your energy there.

As society often conditions us to equate success with wealth, status, or material achievements, disillusionment forces us to question those ideals. Jim Carrey once said, "I wish everyone could get rich and famous so they can see that it's not the answer."

Reframing your goals to focus on what brings you true joy, such as personal relationships, growth, or creative pursuits, can help create a more meaningful and fulfilling path forward.

When disillusionment hit me, it felt like a wave crashing over me. It started with an overwhelming sense of loss—not just of something tangible, but of the very framework I had built my life around. I found myself questioning everything I once held dear. Was the hard work I put in really leading me to happiness? Was the success I sought even worth it?

In times like this, it's crucial to find grounding practices that help you regain a sense of stability.

For me, I turned to my faith. I began praying daily, hoping to find comfort or guidance. For others, this grounding might come from meditation, mindfulness, or spending time in nature—activities that bring a sense of calm and clarity.

Eventually, I started journaling, which made the emotions feel more intense at first, but writing helped me process the overwhelming thoughts swirling in my head. Journaling can be a powerful tool for working through your emotions, giving you an outlet to release frustration and confusion.

Consider setting aside time each day to write about what you're feeling—it doesn't need to be perfect, just honest.

One day, I began going to the park with my kids, sitting under the trees, and just watching them play.

Finding joy in small, simple moments helped me reconnect with the present and allowed me to appreciate life, even when it wasn't perfect.

Spending time in nature or engaging in activities that bring you peace, like reading, cooking, or taking walks, can remind you that life still holds beauty, even when things seem difficult.

This experience with disillusionment changed me. I had always been intense—rushing around, trying to control every detail, worrying about being late or what others thought of me. But after going through disillusionment, I began to see how much of that stress was unnecessary.

> Find a personal mantra or affirmation to help you stay grounded. Remind yourself to let go of what you can't control and focus on what you can.

Letting go of perfectionism is key. Trying to control every little detail will only make you more anxious. Instead, accept that life is unpredictable and messy, and that's okay.

Now, I keep a quote hanging on my wall: "God, grant me the serenity to accept the things I cannot change, the courage to change the things I can, and the wisdom to know the difference."

Disillusionment also helped me become more intentional about my goals. I no longer chase after material things or let

Start by reassessing your priorities.

myself get caught up in the endless pursuit of success.

What truly matters to you? Focus on relationships, personal growth, and activities that align with your values. Cut out mindless distractions, such as excessive social media use, and instead invest time in pursuits that bring you real fulfillment.

Perhaps the most important thing I've learned is that peace comes from within. I used to think that success or external achievements would bring me happiness, but now I know that true peace comes from learning to be content with who you are, regardless of your circumstances. Building self-acceptance and inner resilience will help you weather future disillusionments with more grace and strength.

Disillusionment is difficult, but it can lead to powerful transformation if we allow it to. It forces us to reexamine our beliefs, our goals, and the way we define happiness. The key is to embrace the discomfort and use it as a tool for growth. By focusing on self-compassion, small actions, redefining your values, and letting go of perfectionism, you can find peace in the process.

Learn to accept life's uncertainties, and you'll emerge stronger and more resilient.

Disillusionment isn't the end—it's a chance to rebuild your life with more clarity, purpose, and intention.

CALL TO ACTION

Identify one small action you can take today to move forward and heal from disillusionment.

TIME TO REFLECT

Reflection: How do you typically handle feelings of disappointment or disillusionment?

Reflection: What area of your life is currently challenging your beliefs or expectations?

FINAL TAKEAWAY

Focus on self-compassion, small actions, redefine your values, and let go of perfectionism.

10

The Battle with Despair

Disillusionment has a way of creeping in quietly at first, but when it fully takes hold, it can lead to despair. The harsh realization that the world is not as we once believed can shake us to the core, leaving us with a sense of hopelessness. Despair is more than just sadness or frustration— it's the overwhelming feeling that nothing matters anymore, that life has lost its meaning. When disillusionment hits, it can feel like the world is crumbling around us, and we're left standing alone in the ruins.

Despair is often hard to put into words because it's a deeply personal experience. For some, it might feel like a crushing weight pressing down on them, making it hard to breathe. For others, it might manifest as numbness, a sense of being disconnected from everything and everyone around them. Despair can make you feel like there's no point in trying, no point in hoping, no point in even getting out of bed.

For me, it hit late at night, lying in bed, staring at the ceiling.

It started with a simple thought: "Tomorrow is going to be no different than today." The weight of that thought settled in my chest like a boulder, and before I knew it, I was crying silently, so my kids wouldn't hear. It wasn't just sadness; it was a deep, unshakable sense of emptiness. I felt like I was living the same day over and over again, and it was draining the life out of me.

Replace thoughts of hopelessness with small affirmations to reduce despair's intensity.

The hardest part was how relentless it was. I couldn't shake it. The tears would come out at the most inconvenient times, and I would have to find somewhere to hide, just to let it out. More and more, I felt like I was losing myself, like the person I used to be was slipping away. There were days when I thought about checking myself into a mental health clinic, just to stop the endless cycle of tears and numbness. I didn't want to leave my babies, but I was desperate to feel anything other than what I was feeling.

It wasn't just the sadness, though. There were times when I felt like throwing everything away and being reckless. Normally, I don't drink, I don't smoke, I don't even curse. But in those dark moments, I wanted to let go of all the rules I had built my life around. I wanted to drink, to drown out the sorrow, even though I knew it wouldn't help. The desire to escape was so strong. I understood, in a way I never had before, why people turn to these things. I sympathized with those who tried to cope by drowning their pain at the bottom of a bottle.

Despair is a universal experience, one that can stem from numerous sources—loss, failure, or the realization that life doesn't align with our expectations. Mental health experts often emphasize the importance of seeking support during these dark times, whether through therapy, spiritual guidance, or simply reaching out to a trusted friend. While it may feel like an insurmountable burden, despair can be managed by breaking it into smaller steps. Practices like mindfulness, grounding techniques, and establishing daily routines can offer some relief. It's important to remember that despair doesn't last forever; even the darkest moments will eventually pass.

Seek spiritual connection to help process emotions and find moments of peace.

But because of my kids, I didn't. I couldn't. Even when I felt like I was unraveling, the thought of them kept me from going too far. I just sat there in my car, my foot propped on the dashboard, staring out the window, and let the tears flow freely. I felt trapped between wanting to give in to the darkness and knowing I had to keep it together for them.

For a long time, I didn't know how to get out of that place. I would go through the motions, especially on the days that mattered, like birthdays or family events. I'd smile and act like everything was fine, but inside, I was falling apart. The real turning point came when I began telling myself: "I'm almost done crying." I didn't believe it at first, but I kept saying it. After a few days, I changed the thought to: "I'm not going to cry today." Eventually, I made it to, "I am done crying."

While the emotional impact was significant, the real shift came through conscious self-talk. Gradually replacing thoughts of hopelessness with small affirmations helped reduce despair's intensity.

Allow yourself to grieve.

It wasn't a magical fix, but gradually, I started to come out of that dark place. It was painful, and there were days I felt like I was taking two steps forward and one step back. But little by little, I began to heal.

What helped me the most, though, was praying. I prayed every day, asking God for guidance, for comfort, for anything that could bring me peace. There were moments when I felt like God was the only one listening. Even when I couldn't feel joy, I found some peace in prayer. Talking to God helped me release the emotions I couldn't share with anyone else, knowing He understood, even when I didn't. That connection, that faith, was the biggest help in pulling me through.

Seeking spiritual connection helped provide a form of relief that was inaccessible through other means. It allowed for processing emotions and finding moments of peace.

Over time, I started to learn that I was stronger than I thought. I found power in my mind. I had talked myself down from so many dark places, and I realized that if I hadn't, I didn't know where I would be. Writing became a huge part of my healing process. Journaling every day helped me face my emotions head-on. There were days I was scared I'd never find my way back—that I would never get over the painful truths that had shaken my world. But slowly, I started to see that there was life beyond despair.

It was one of the hardest experiences of my life, but I'm on the other side now. I felt isolated through the whole process, like I couldn't tell anyone because who would understand? I went through it alone, but I don't recommend that at all. If I could do it over again, I would have reached out more. But I made it through, and now, I'm stronger because of it.

Allowing myself to grieve and write helped me take control over my emotions, helping me heal one step at a time.

Recognize that emotions are temporary.
Despair is not permanent.

Despair can feel all-consuming, but it's not permanent. Through faith, reflection, and small, consistent actions, it is possible to regain a sense of control and purpose. Despair often comes from feeling stuck, but the path to healing begins when you acknowledge your emotions and take steps toward recovery. By embracing the process and recognizing that emotions are temporary, you can learn to navigate even the darkest moments, emerging stronger and more resilient.

CALL TO ACTION

Journal a moment when you overcame despair and what you learned from it.

TIME TO REFLECT

Reflection: How do you cope with feelings of despair in your daily life?

Reflection: What has been your most significant source of strength in overcoming dark moments?

FINAL TAKEAWAY

Strength comes from facing your darkest emotions and realizing "you can make it."

Section Three

Embracing Change and Resilience

"Your journey is a process of becoming,
and each truth you uncover leads you
closer to who you truly are."

—Unknown

11

Awareness and Acceptance

Disillusionment, for all the pain and confusion it brings, can serve as a gateway to deeper awareness. When the beliefs we've clung to shatter and the world we thought we knew feels foreign, we're forced to wake up and see things as they truly are. This is a difficult and often unwelcome process, but it's necessary for growth.

Illusions, whether in relationships, career goals, or success, shield us from truth. It's only when they crack that we begin to understand reality.

The Reality Check: A Personal Story

I remember the first time I truly accepted that things weren't as I thought. It was after coming out of a long relationship that had consumed years of my energy and emotions. I had invested so much, hoping it would bring happiness and fulfillment, but it didn't. Deep down, I knew things weren't right, but I held on because I believed love could fix everything.

I didn't want to accept that I had been wrong.

When the relationship ended, I was left with a void. It wasn't just the breakup that hurt—it was realizing I had been holding onto a false sense of security.

I was in denial, believing that trying harder would make everything fall into place.

That was the first time I became aware of how much of my life had been built on ideas that weren't real.

Acceptance didn't come easily. At first, I was angry—angry at the situation and at myself for believing in something false. But as months passed, I began to see that this experience was forcing me to grow.

I had to accept that love alone doesn't fix everything, and that not all relationships are meant to last.

That awareness shifted how I viewed not just relationships, but myself. I became more in tune with what I needed, learning that sometimes, letting go of illusions is the only way forward.

Disillusionment Brings Clarity

Disillusionment forces us to confront reality head-on, pushing us toward acceptance. We start to see that the ideals we held, whether about love, success, or happiness, were based on false promises. This awareness feels like a burden at first, as it strips away the comfort of naivety, but it is a powerful tool for growth.

Once you see things clearly, you can't pretend anymore. You must confront your flaws, the flaws of others, and the imperfections of the world around you.

One uncomfortable truth I had to accept was that not everything in life is within my control. For someone who prided themselves on planning and anticipating every outcome, this was a harsh lesson. No matter how hard I worked, there would always be factors beyond my control. This was disheartening, but it eventually brought me peace. I learned to focus on what I could control and let go of the rest.

Awareness as a Path to Growth

The awareness that comes with disillusionment can feel overwhelming, but it opens the door to change. Each time I've confronted uncomfortable truths, whether about relationships, career paths, or my limitations, I came out stronger.

Awareness allows you to make informed choices and live authentically.

The Price of Denial

The flip side of awareness is denial, which feels easier because it allows us to stay in comfortable situations, but denial leads to stagnation. When we refuse to face reality, we stay stuck, repeating patterns and wondering why things don't change. It wasn't until I faced these truths head-on that I realized growth lies in awareness, not in clinging to false hopes.

Embracing Acceptance

Acceptance means letting go of fantasies and ideals that keep us stuck. It means acknowledging that life won't always work out as we want, and that's okay.

Acceptance doesn't mean giving up—it means making peace with reality to build a better future.

For me, acceptance was a gradual process. I had to let go of the belief that my life had to follow a specific path, and that if I tried harder, things would always go my way.

As I learned to accept these truths, I found freedom.

I stopped worrying about what I couldn't control and started focusing on what I could. I became more present in my daily life, appreciating small moments of joy.

The Gift of Disillusionment

In the end, disillusionment gave me something more valuable than the illusions I lost. It gave me clarity. It showed me what truly matters and helped me live in a way more aligned with my values. Disillusionment is painful, but if you can accept the truth and learn from it, it leads to a deeper, more meaningful way of living.

Awareness and acceptance go hand in hand. Awareness allows us to see the truth, and acceptance helps us live in harmony with it. Together, they empower us to grow, to let go of what no longer serves us, and to embrace life as it is. Though challenging, this process leads to greater peace, purpose, and fulfillment.

CALL TO ACTION

Reflect on one truth you've learned recently and how you can embrace it moving forward.

TIME TO REFLECT

Reflection: What truths have you had to accept about your life?

Reflection: How has awareness of these truths led to personal growth?

FINAL TAKEAWAY

Let go of what no longer serves you, and to embrace life as it is.

12

Rewriting the Narrative: Authentic Living and Meaning

Disillusionment is something most of us will face at some point in our lives. Whether it comes from shattered expectations, broken dreams, or a painful realization about the world, it forces us to confront the uncomfortable truths we've been avoiding. But once you get through it, disillusionment offers something invaluable: the opportunity to rewrite your own narrative and live more authentically.

Before disillusionment hit me, I lived by a script I didn't even realize I was following. The milestones of adulthood—success, relationships, material wealth—were all laid out in front of me like a checklist, and I was doing my best to mark off each one. I thought I knew what I wanted, but the truth is, most of my goals were built on societal expectations rather than my own desires. I believed that if I achieved these things, I would be happy.

I thought success meant having a good career, a picture-perfect relationship, and financial stability. But life doesn't always go according to plan, and disillusionment revealed that those ideals weren't as fulfilling as I had been led to believe.

When you're forced to confront the fact that life isn't what you thought it would be, it can be devastating. The dreams you once clung to feel distant and hollow. But once the initial shock wears off, disillusionment offers a chance to rebuild. It's an invitation to take a closer look at what truly matters to you and to live in a way that feels authentic and meaningful.

One of the biggest shifts I experienced was in how I defined success. For so long, I equated success with external achievements. I thought if I worked hard enough, reached a certain income, or achieved a specific title, I'd be fulfilled.

But when disillusionment set in, I realized that those things alone wouldn't bring me peace. I had been striving for a version of success that was based on other people's definitions, not mine.

I've had to redefine success on my own terms. Now, it's not about how much money I make or how many accolades I collect. It's about how fulfilled I feel at the end of each day.

Love is another area where my disillusionment shifted my perspective. For a long time, I believed in the idealized version of love that we see in movies—the kind of love that sweeps you off your feet and makes everything feel perfect.

But real love is far more complex. It's not about perfection or fairy tales. It's about showing up, day after day, even when it's hard. It's about choosing each other through the ups and downs and understanding that love doesn't always look the way we expect it to.

By shifting how I defined love, I learned that real love is found in consistency, effort, and mutual support, not in fleeting perfection.

Life doesn't always unfold according to plan, but

disillusionment provides an opportunity to redefine your personal narrative. By letting go of societal expectations and focusing on what truly brings you joy and fulfillment, you can rewrite your story in a way that aligns with your authentic self.

Success is not about external achievements but about living in alignment with your values. The power to create a meaningful and fulfilling life lies in your hands—through intentional choices and self-acceptance.

CALL TO ACTION

Journal a moment when you overcame despair and what you learned from it.

TIME TO REFLECT

Reflection: What is one area of your life where you've been following someone else's script?

Reflection: How can you begin rewriting that narrative today?

FINAL TAKEAWAY

Set one intentional goal that aligns with your authentic self—whether it's related to your career, relationships, or personal development.

13

Embracing the Journey Ahead

As you've journeyed through these pages, you've witnessed the highs and lows, the joy and the pain that come with disillusionment, love, loss, and growth. The stories and reflections shared here are not just mine—they reflect universal truths that we all encounter at some point in life. We've all faced moments where the world doesn't make sense, where our hopes have been shattered, and where we've had to rebuild from the ruins of our expectations. But here's the secret: these moments, as difficult as they are, are also opportunities.

Disillusionment is not the end—it's a new beginning.

It strips away the illusions and false promises that we've been holding onto, and in doing so, it frees us to live more authentically. When we let go of what no longer serves us, we make space for something better, something truer.

The road ahead won't always be easy. The process of letting go, of accepting reality for what it is, takes time and courage. But it's in that very space—between what was and what is—that we find our greatest strength. We learn that we don't have to have all the answers. Life doesn't have to follow a certain script. And most importantly, it's okay to not be okay all the time.

Now, as you move forward, this is your opportunity to put the lessons of this book into practice.

At the end of each chapter, there are reflection questions designed to help you dig deeper into your own experiences. Take the time to revisit those questions, reflect honestly, and use the Personal Action Plan template in the appendix to start making tangible changes in your life. This is your moment to take action, to set new goals based on the truths you've uncovered about yourself, and to create a plan that aligns with who you are, not who you think you should be.

The truth is, life is messy.

It's unpredictable, imperfect, and sometimes unfair. But within that mess lies meaning. It's in the struggles, the setbacks, and the heartbreaks that we learn what truly matters. We learn who we are, what we value, and how we want to live. We begin to shape our lives, not based on societal expectations, but on our own truth and inner compass.

As you move forward, here's how to take the next step:

Start Small: Identify one area of your life where you feel disillusioned or stuck. Use the reflection questions and Personal Action Plan to explore this area, and outline one or two small actions you can take to begin moving forward.

Focus on Progress, Not Perfection: Remember, change doesn't happen overnight. The goal is to start shifting your mindset and actions toward what truly matters to you, not to achieve immediate results.

Embrace Accountability: Share your plan with a trusted friend or loved one who can support you on this journey. Accountability will help keep you on track and motivated.

Review and Revise: As you start to implement your plan, take time to review your progress regularly. Adjust your goals as needed, and don't be afraid to pivot if something no longer feels aligned with your true self.

By taking these steps, you can begin to transform your disillusionment into growth, your pain into purpose, and your uncertainty into clarity.

You are stronger than you know.

You've already survived so much, and you will continue to grow with each new challenge that comes your way. This journey is ongoing, and the lessons we learn along the way shape who we become. There will be more ups and downs, but remember: you've already proven that you can make it through the darkest of moments.

In the end, life isn't about achieving perfection or checking off a list of accomplishments. It's about finding peace in the present moment, about cultivating relationships that nourish your soul, and about living in a way that feels true to you. Let that be your guide as you continue your journey forward.

Thank you for walking this path with me. As we both continue on our separate journeys, may we find the strength to keep growing, the courage to embrace the unknown, and the grace to accept ourselves exactly as we are.

CALL TO ACTION
Write out a new narrative for yourself, focusing on the next chapter of your life.

Appendix

One-Year Action Plan

One of my favorite quotes to remember is: "Doing the same thing and expecting a different result is the definition of insanity" — attributed to Albert Einstein (though it has not been fully proven). Nevertheless, this quote raises a good point. So many times, we wonder why things in our life always turn out the same way, but we rarely stop to look at the full picture or examine what led to those results.

The best advice I could give anyone (especially because it worked for me) is to give yourself a full year of doing things completely differently from the way you have been doing them. Below, you will find a breakdown of an action plan that, if used correctly, could help you to plan out your year and change your life for the better.

One-Year Action Plan

Step 1: In your calendar, go to the date that is exactly one year from now and write the words, "Look at where you are now." Doing this will open your eyes to one of three things: either you'll be better than you are now, worse, or in the same position. The choice is entirely yours to make from here, but this is a way to hold yourself accountable and track your progress.

Step 2: Write out your ideal life. What does life look like when you have achieved everything you want?

Step 3: Write out how you plan to get there. Do you want a career? How much do you want to make? What field is this career in? What do you have to learn?

Step 4: Write out, in as much detail as you can, why you want it. Your "why" will keep you motivated when it gets hard — because it will.

Step 5: Create a routine that involves taking small actions that move you closer to your goal. Little steps help keep you from becoming overwhelmed and keep you moving forward.

Step 6: Celebrate your wins, big and small. Doing this will help you gain awareness of what you are doing that can help or hinder your goals.

Step 7: Write down your long-term, short-term, and daily goals. Do this often. Keeping your goals top of mind will help you remember to work toward them.

These are simple steps that can help you create a different outcome for your life than what you have been experiencing. Disillusionment does not have to make your life feel pointless. For me personally, it has opened my eyes to the many opportunities I might have missed if I'd stayed on the path that was laid out for me. Aim for freedom, not perfection, because perfection is not the goal.

ABOUT THE AUTHOR

Olivia L. Harris has always been a storyteller at heart, her vivid imagination drawing her into the worlds of books, movies, and TV shows from a young age. In contrast to her quiet demeanor in real life, she found her true voice on the page, where she could express herself freely. Becoming a published author was a dream she nurtured for years but often avoided out of fear—fear of failure and the pressure of living up to the praise of those around her. Writing this book allowed her to confront those fears and discover her own inner strength.

Olivia holds a master's degree in marketing and several certifications in technology. By day, she works as a full-time Salesforce developer while raising her children, but her passion for writing remains ever-present. When she's not writing or working, she enjoys losing herself in a good book, listening to jazz music, and soaking in the peacefulness of rainy days.

www.ingramcontent.com/pod-product-compliance
Lightning Source LLC
Chambersburg PA
CBHW060445040426
42331CB00044B/2614